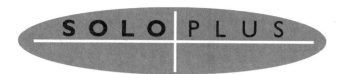

SOLO PLUS

B & T KEYBOARDS
£ 9.95

Alto Saxophone

with piano accompaniment

An outstanding collection of classic Christmas tunes
expertly arranged for the beginning soloist with piano accompaniment
in printed *and* digitally recorded formats.

GW00599558

Amsco Publications
New York/London/Paris/Sydney/Copenhagen/Madrid

Cover photography by Randall Wallace
Arranged and performed by David Pearl

This book Copyright © 2000 by Amsco Publications,
A Division of Music Sales Corporation, New York

All rights reserved. No part of this book may be
reproduced in any form or by any electronic or mechanical means,
including information storage and retrieval systems,
without permission in writing from the publisher.

Order No. AM 967571
US International Standard Book Number: 0.8256.1817.7
UK International Standard Book Number: 0.7119.8513.8

Exclusive Distributors:
Music Sales Corporation
257 Park Avenue South, New York, NY 10010 USA
Music Sales Limited
8/9 Frith Street, London W1D 3JB England
Music Sales Pty. Limited
120 Rothschild Street, Rosebery, Sydney, NSW 2018, Australia

Printed in the United States of America by
Vicks Lithograph and Printing Corporation

Contents

Angels We Have Heard on High

Traditional French carol

Moderately fast (♩ = 120)

Copyright © 2000 by Music Sales Corporation (ASCAP)
International Copyright Secured. All Rights Reserved.

to Coda ⊕

D.S. al Coda ⊕

⊕ Coda

allarg.

allarg.

8-ל

Deck the Hall

Traditional Welsh carol

Copyright © 2000 by Music Sales Corporation (ASCAP)
International Copyright Secured. All Rights Reserved.

The First Noel

Traditional English carol

Copyright © 2000 by Music Sales Corporation (ASCAP)
International Copyright Secured. All Rights Reserved.

It Came Upon a Midnight Clear

Richard Storrs Willis (1819–1900)

Copyright © 2000 by Music Sales Corporation (ASCAP)
International Copyright Secured. All Rights Reserved.

Go, Tell It on the Mountain

Traditional African-American spiritual

Copyright © 2000 by Music Sales Corporation (ASCAP)
International Copyright Secured. All Rights Reserved.

God Rest Ye Merry, Gentlemen

Traditional English carol

Moderately bright (♩ = 69)

Copyright © 2000 by Music Sales Corporation (ASCAP)
International Copyright Secured. All Rights Reserved.

I Wonder as I Wander

John Jacob Niles (1892–1980)

Copyright © 1934 (Renewed) by G. Schirmer,Inc. (ASCAP)
International Copyright Secured. All Rights Reserved.
Reprinted by Permission.

Jingle Bells

James S. Pierpont (1822–1893)

Copyright © 2000 by Music Sales Corporation (ASCAP)
International Copyright Secured. All Rights Reserved.

O Come, All Ye Faithful

Adeste Fidelis

Traditional English carol

Copyright © 2000 by Music Sales Corporation (ASCAP)
International Copyright Secured. All Rights Reserved.

O, Holy Night

Adolphe Adam (1803–1856)

Copyright © 2000 by Music Sales Corporation (ASCAP)
International Copyright Secured. All Rights Reserved.

O Little Town of Bethlehem

Lewis H. Redner (1831–1908)

Copyright © 2000 by Music Sales Corporation (ASCAP)
International Copyright Secured. All Rights Reserved.

The Babe of Bethle'm

Traditional English carol

Copyright © 2000 by Music Sales Corporation (ASCAP)
International Copyright Secured. All Rights Reserved.

Silent Night

Franz X. Gruber (1787–1863)

Moderately slow (♪ = 76)

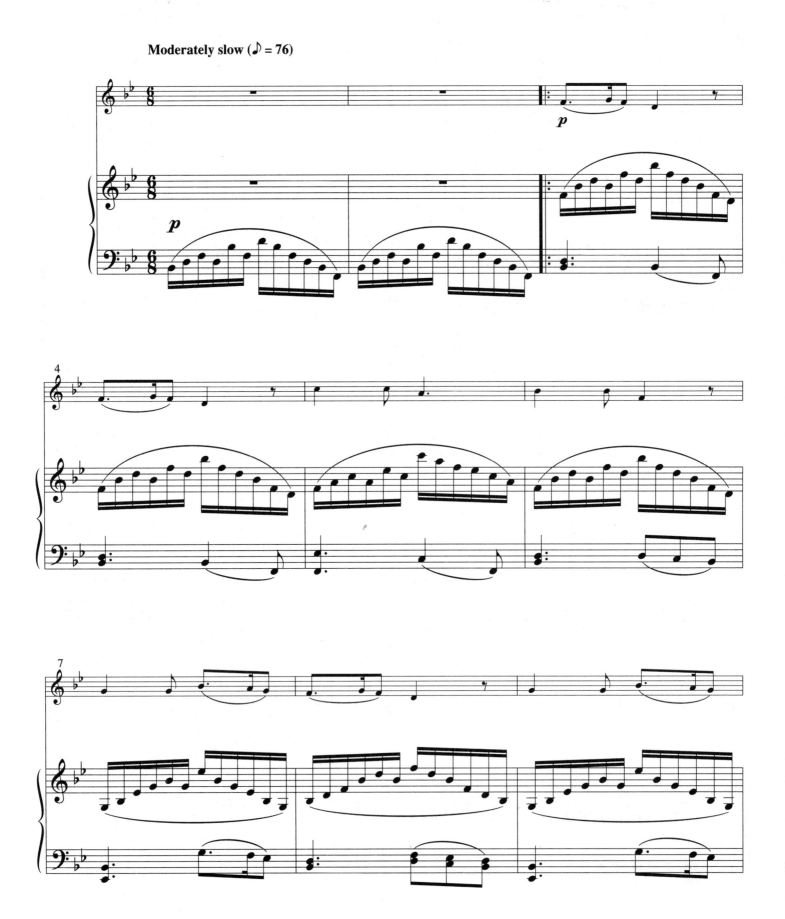

Copyright © 2000 by Music Sales Corporation (ASCAP)
International Copyright Secured. All Rights Reserved.

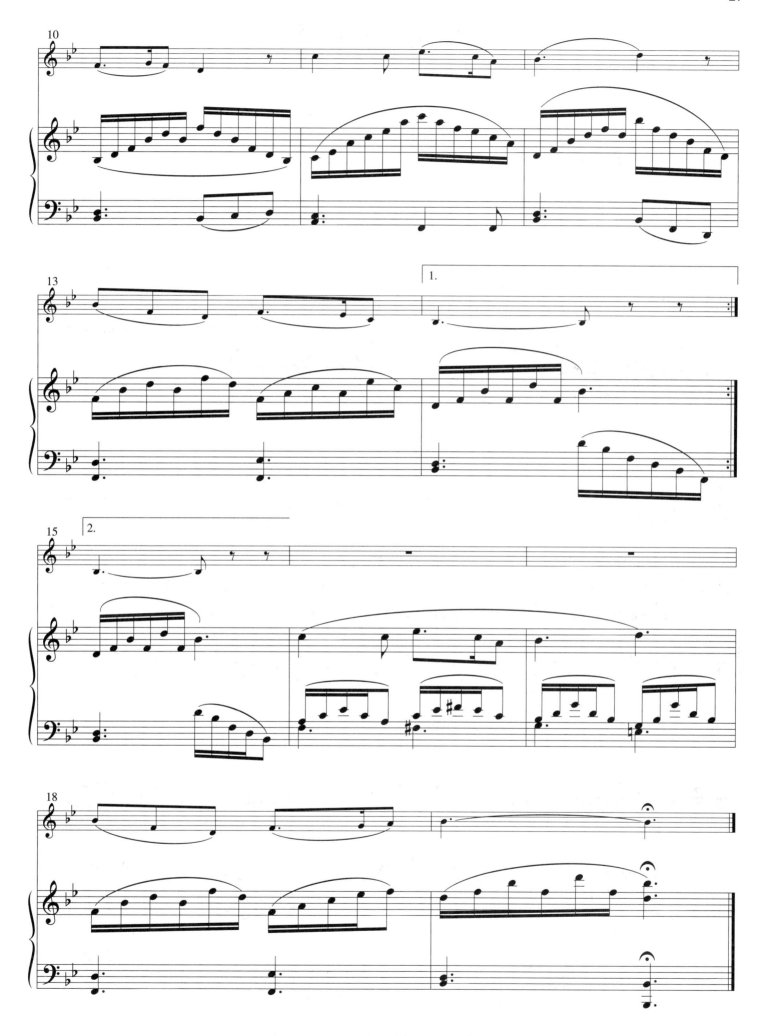

What Child Is This?

Greensleeves

Traditional English air

Copyright © 2000 by Music Sales Corporation (ASCAP)
International Copyright Secured. All Rights Reserved.

Rocking

Traditional Czech carol

Copyright © 2000 by Music Sales Corporation (ASCAP)
International Copyright Secured. All Rights Reserved.